AGUA SANTA

HOLY WATER

Camino del Sol

A LATINA AND LATINO LITERARY SERIES

Pat Mora

Agua Santa
Holy Water

The University of Arizona Press

Tucson

The University of Arizona Press
© 1995 by Pat Mora
First University of Arizona Press paperbound printing 2007

Library of Congress Cataloging-in-Publication Data
Mora, Pat.
  Agua santa = Holy water / Pat Mora.
    p. cm. – (Camino del sol)
ISBN 978-0-8165-2663-5 (pbk. : acid-free paper)
    1. Mexican American women—Poetry. 2. Mexican Americans—
Poetry. I. Title. II. Title: Holy water.
PS3563.073A72 2007
811'.54—dc22   2007003802

Manufactured in the United States of America on acid-free,
archival-quality paper.

12 11 10 09 08 07   6 5 4 3 2 1

Agua Santa = Holy Water was originally published in 1995
by Beacon Press, Boston, Mass.

for

VERN SCARBOROUGH

treasured water scholar

CONTENTS

ACKNOWLEDGMENTS

My thanks to the editors of the publications in which versions of the following poems previously appeared: "Dear Frida" in *Mid-American Review*; "Los brazos del rio" in *Indiana Review*; "La Migra" in *Ms.*; "The Loving Strip" and "Depression Days" in *Texas Poetry Anthology*; "Pescadote" in *New Chicana/Chicano Writing 2*; "Agua negra," "Nunca, nunca," and "It May Be Dangerous" in *New Chicana/Chicano Writing 3*; "Tzimin Chaak" in *Unsettling America: Race and Ethnicity in Contemporary American Literature*; "Cuentista" and "Cuidado" in *Footwork: The Paterson Literary Review*; "Sly Woman" and "Cuban Revolutionary" in *Paper Dance: 55 Latino Poets*; "Sueño de miel" in *Colorado Review*; "Doña Feliciana," "Tornabé," and "La dulcería" in *In Other Words: Literature by Latina Writers of the United States*; "The Shadow," "Spring Shining," "Mangos y limones," and "Coatlicue's Rules: Advice from an Aztec Goddess" in *Prairie Schooner*.

I also wish to thank Jane Flanders, Norma Jenckes, and Murray Bodo for their advice on many of the poems. A special thanks to my enthusiastic editor, Deborah Chasman, and to Murray (again) and Sandra Cisneros who took the time to read and give advice on the entire manuscript.

I deeply appreciate a fellowship from the National Endowment for the Arts that allowed the final editing.

OLD SEA

The Loving Strip

1

Not for men alone do we remove our clothes,
slowly unbutton ourselves and stare
at flesh soft as the underside of petals.

2

The aunt who dressed in black knew how to laugh,
but her scowling tongue ticked, *t-t, t-t, t-t,*
each time Rock Hudson pressed his lips on Doris Day.

We'd jab Lobo hard, embarrassed at her
muttered "¡Válgame Dios! ¡Válgame Dios!"
but every Sunday: movies' luscious dark.

Afterwards, the depot, trains chugging out,
hand-in-hand walk to the plaza and Salvation
Army time. She knew. I loved that thumping drum.

Lobo's tongue ticked *t-t, t-t, t-t* at every man,
but she could melt our frowns. Daily
she brought Archie comics, Butterfingers.

Late at night, she lifted her hand above
our bodies, "La cruz más grande del mundo."
Her blessing, a sturdy, familiar quilt.

3

Always in black, Lobo never wore slacks,
a lady of high collars, sleeves to her wrists.
Of course, she didn't swim

until the day our tears removed her clothes.
The pool sign: No bathing without an adult.
She read our sighs. (Not for men alone

do we remove our clothes.)
She rented a black bathing suit, two-piece.
Though I was there, all that flesh and her face

will never match, and yet, I hear her laugh.
We splash, climb her, dive into ripples green,
circle, like frisky seals around our rock.

Ofrenda for Lobo

Come, fierce guardian angel
in black shoes. Let me whet
your appetite. I've gathered
all you loved, or still love,
for this *altar*, tiers of sweet
temptation, earth's delights.
Visit me, if only for a night.

Come. Papel picado sways to guitars
white as starlight on this arch in bloom.
Velvet scents have I for you, champagne
mists of pale perfumes, crimson petals,
green of pine, coiling clouds: countless
candles, burning, burning bright on this
altar to whet your stubborn appetite.
Drift back. Visit me if only for tonight.

Come. Sweet steam invites: café, camote en leche.
Melodies polite curl round you soft as this smoke
at midnight. Follow: click of rosary beads, rumors
of agua santa. Bite bread, white for our communion,
shaped like a wolf, you, head tense, shielding her cubs.
Come, books to lure you to recite old tales, and we
will reunite in cuentos of ancestors who rise at dawn,
lift their voices in songs of praise. Like wise incense
your words rise, coil, whet your appetite; entangle
you, entangle me. Come. Visit, if only for this night.

Oasis

To avoid the sting,
our good-byes,
I hide in rose-scented pages,
the fabled gardens
of Persia,
like you, oasis
from the glare.

Arcs of light
dart through poppies
like glinting fish.
Water sings crystal
flights in fountains,
streams tile-lined canals into white
petaled breaths: orange blossoms,
jasmine, into scarlet
incense, roses coiling
their velvet spell.

Shade plays
in the throats
of callas, drowses in the rustle,
butterfly arabesques
over rippled reflections,
cypress, willows, palms.

Icy afternoon wine,
geranium and lime
sherbets melt into us
as we see through ourselves

in pools, murmur
philosophies of wings.

Palms drum the sun
to rest. Lingering nightingale
song, *gulbang*, flower cry,
darkens the juice
of pomegranates,
the tulips' perfume.

Among a thousand scattered
rose petals—our fragrant,
crimson sky—candles float,
like stars, like you.

Ballena

Are you terrified of drowning?
   Bleeding, you flee, hurl
      yourself toward land, air, that strange
         sand to which we cling, seres del desierto
            who can't remember our wet beginning.

Are you terrified of drowning,
   crusted arc vaulting your heaviness
      from the blue womb into a gasp,
         knower of densest roots who smashes ships
            like pomegranates, splatter of blood, seeds.

These fathoms, home, yours and your babies'.
   In you slide, deep into hymns,
      el canto hondo. With no vocal cords,
         you all sing the same song,
            the sea pressing you to rise again.

We wait
   to see your fist of an eye,
      a creature who sings
         where it can't breathe.

Another Brown Man

Startling as blood
from a pinprick,
my tears, pull
me to him, away from hipsway,
drumbeats, música cubana.

His hands, like yours,
the color of tobacco
he smooths, cuts, rolls,
another brown man,
hands and humor busy. Like yours.

His chuckles curl with his cigar smoke,
his teases to girls in nearby shops,
"Oye, linda,"
banter familiar as the work,
rhythm I remember.

> You stopped breathing
> once this year. Your body,
> solid as an álamo,
> we can never trust again.
> It practiced stillness.

I stare at him, hover
near music I once knew,
listen, hear you
whose voice alone
pricks my tears.

I turn, and he's gone,
light off, cigar rolling done for the day,
his spot bare under the palm trees,
only a shadow.
Like yours.

The Shadow

Tapping. On the window an insistent
   tapping, rain pulling me from sleep,
no, not rain,
   a shadow on the ceiling. Wings.

A black butterfly, the rising slow
   like an eagle, flying into my dream, leading me
down a rolling hill to a field of small suns,
   steamy yellow and white wildflowers. Sleep.

A fluttering, like book pages flapping wildly
   around the bed, no,   wings,
the summer a snake twitched in the watering can.
   Bead eyes peered at me, speechless tongue,
slither I poured into the grass.

The shadow
   on the ceiling, a shape older than memory
smelling of caves not fields, of death, teeth, blood,
   the furred center, flying mouth open, through my house.

All day the sightless body hid, hung
   in some dark space in the kitchen, dreaming
as coffee brewed, of spreading its full self,
   at dusk gliding blackness again through every room.

I didn't hear, though they did warn me,
   those dark, kindly creatures, the summer my father died.

Corazón del corrido

1
En la frontera de Tejas,
miren lo que ha sucedido,
venían los mexicanos,
buscaban lo prometido.

2
En mil novecientos quince,
de Chihuahua Moras llegaban,
buscaban paz pa' sus hijos,
al Paso Norte mudaban.

3
Venía Raúl Antonio,
llegó de niño chiquito,
a siete ya trabajaba,
lechero con caballito.

4
Buscaba otro trabajo,
periódicos él vendía,
después de ir a la escuela,
tantas tareas tenía.

5
De chico iba a los pleitos,
—Soy de la prensa, decía,
en periódicos se sentaba,
gran boxeadores veía.

6

Jugetón desde muy joven,
a su hermana asustaba,
vestido en sábana blanca,
como espanto gritaba.

7

Su padre, sastre paciente,
su madre nunca paraba,
esa familia tan grande,
Raúl lo necesitaba.

8

Decía Raúl Antonio,
y sin pistola en la mano,
y sin caballo melado,
—Soy luchador mexicano.

9

Un hombre bien aplicado,
gerente pues lo nombraban,
su sueldo daba a su madre,
amigos lo admiraban.

10

Pero llegaban los güeros,
que ojos malos le daban.
—Jamás podrán insultarme,
¡Adiós! Ya no lo abusaban.

11

—¿Qué haré? pensaba ese joven,
cuando lavaba su coche,

—Te ocupo, dijo un viandante.
—Iré al taller día y noche.

12

Los lentes bien él pulía,
y las medidas tomaba.
—¡Muchachos, prisa! gritaba.
Ni pa' comidas paraba.

13

A veces dando un paseo,
bonita joven veía,
sentada frente a su casa,
—¡Qué linda! Raúl decía.

14

—Con esa voy a casarme.
Pronto con ella salía,
mandaba muchos regalos,
y ella se sonreía.

15

Esposo de bella Estella,
de piedra casa fincaron,
y cuatro hijos tuvieron,
los cuatro bien educaron.

16

Fue dueño de su negocio,
al pobre siempre ayudaba,
por años de día y noche,
los lentes él trabajaba.

17

Decía Raúl Antonio,
y sin pistola en la mano,
—Yo cuidaré a mi familia,
Soy luchador mexicano.

18

Al fin las cuentas montaban,
se fue buscando dinero,
a Houston, Gallup, Califas,
se mudó entre el güero.

19

Jugetón desde muy joven,
con nietos siempre guasaba,
les daba pues su domingo,
y luego los pellizcaba.

20

¡Ay! Murió en California,
y sin pistola en la mano,
y sin caballo melado,
gran luchador mexicano.

21

Aquí se acaba el corrido,
y como él lucharemos,
ya con ésta me despido,
¡Ay, Papá! te cantaremos.

for my father

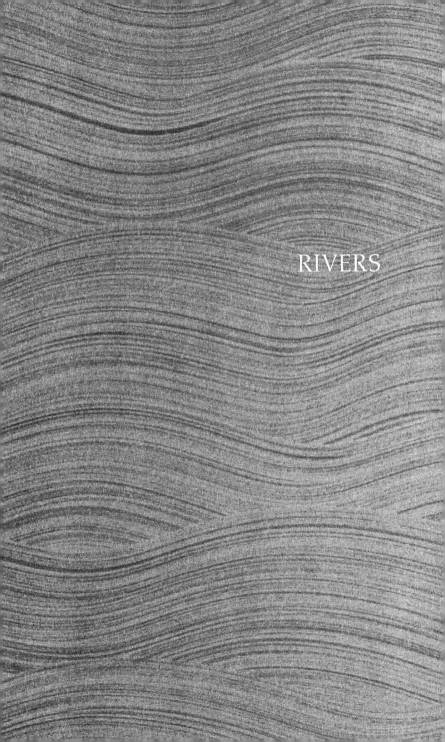

RIVERS

Aurelia: Moon Jellies

Without brain or eye or heart,
    Aurelia bud,
join in a sea of chance,
   attach to solid surfaces:
    coral or rock;
      in caverns, clone,
        then float free
          like ruffled seaflowers.

Without brain or eye or heart,
    Aurelia furl,
skin slight as a sigh,
   propel themselves, hidden
    in watery night.
      They tumble and doze.
        Like weightless glass bells
         they gather light, glow.

Without brain or eye or heart,
    Aurelia drift,
bodies transparent as embryos.
   Tentacles trailing,
    they ride unseen
      currents, bathed by all they need
       in agua santa, old sea,
        depths where we begin.

A Child, a Child

You held your breath
for months it seemed,
feared each phone ring,
her voice saying,
"Can't give you this baby."

Then the unexpected:
    "Breech."
Together, you sat the hours
    the baby in her
heavy between his mothers,

oblivious, as children often are,
of the talking, tears
not new to either of you,
hers, resignation,
this parting, final,
yours, fear so loud
you strained to hear her words.

Four mother hands
held him those first days,
and you watched her every move,
knew it was you she held.

The last day there was talk
of love, and she placed him
in your arms. Privately, you
altered fate, woman-to-woman.

Your mouth formed that new word,
son, and his breath began slipping into you,
warm, steady, those breaths,
tiny puffs filling you,
like those Japanese streamers
flown on Boy's Day Festival,
carp banners, hardy fish
that charge upstream,
good male spirit.

Good spirit, I say, yours,
those babybreaths filling
you. Your joy streaming forth proclaiming
at long last, let the celebration begin.

Mama Spell

Leave your storyless books, you three,
Leave your storyless books.
Come and join in the dance, you three,
Night is calling your names, you three,
Night is calling your names.
Come dance in the light of the moon, *toon-toon*.
Come dance in the light of the moon.

Toss your sensible shoes, my three,
Toss your sensible shoes.
Shake your hips till the glee returns
For mischief sails through the night, you three,
Bats, owls, witches, devils,
Will dance in the light of the moon, *whoo-whoo*,
Will dance in the light of the moon.

Wear these masks for escape, my three,
Masks I shaped with great care.
Cats you'll be in your private dance,
Three dancing cats you'll be, *hee-hee*,
Three dancing cats you'll be.
You'll pounce in the light of the moon, *toon-toon*,
Reunite in the light of the moon.

A tigre can you be, my son,
Bristles, tusks, eyes on fire,
Growl and roar, O fierce night cat,
Glare from wood mask black and yellow.
Come prowl the rhythm of drums,

Discover your hidden nagual, *pan-pan*,
Come, dance in the fright of the moon.

Hide in this mesh mask, strong daughter,
Peer from eyes darkly lashed.
Here, jubilant plumed hat for you,
Feathered rainbow to catch their eye,
Spin, fly, most privately,
Unforgettable cat you'll be, *hee-hee*,
As you dance in the sight of the moon.

Mask as round as the moon, last child,
Globe of gold papier-mâché,
Grin inside the layers, *toon-toon*,
Ribbons, bells on your kitten face,
Music you bring, so prance,
Ta-lán, Ta-lán, Tan-tán, Ta-lán.
Come dance, delight this moony moon.

I'll sit in a tree, watch you three,
Playing like long ago,
Three different cats you be, *hee-hee*,
Freed by the masks to dance your dance,
Drums, rattles call your names,
Prance with your spirits, my three, *hee-hee*,
Come. Dance in the light of the moon.

Halloween 1993

Braided

Rain, rattle of shells
                    outside my window. "Listen,"
you'd whisper small finger to lips,
                    curled in your nest of sheets,
desert wind whirring, rocking branches
                    round our house. "Listen. Outside
my window. Indians. Dancing."

Eyes closed, even here among Ohio maples and oaks,
                    I hear those spirits return, gather,
their moccasins drumming outside my window,
                    unbroken music, muffled by leaves.

They return, the whispered mother/daughter murmurs
                    in the rooms we flowed through,
año tras año, braiding our voices.
                    an invisible but audible strand,
rhythm old as crooning *rru-rru-rru*
                    into the downy ear of a newborn,

the braiding like rivers, their flowings
                    and gatherings, spilling into one another,
echoes rippling through currents, crossing, crisscrossing.

for Cissy

The Weight of a Life

The darting comet streaks in
and out of your breaths,
bones like small chopsticks
under long, white fur, and a heart—
no bigger than a strawberry—
outraces yours. For the first time,
you feel the weight, life in your hands.

I had a friend afraid to plant
even marigolds. Her babies kept slipping out
when they were smaller
than your kitten.
She feared her hands were dangerous.

Remember your sister's fish tank
empty and silent for months?
To end her tears
at every fish that died,
we poured the risk
away. The tank shrank.
Without the glints, the music ceased,

the stillness heavy
like hands that forget
how to let another float within the palms.

for Libby

The Lure

"The octopus on the platter moved."

I remember your first crawlings
after all you sensed, lizards whipping through
grass, and whispering specks, spiders
we could hardly see. Later, arms open wide
you pursued the lure, Painted Ladies, Monarchs,
for an instant felt life flutter in your palms.

"The octopus on the platter moved."

At four, you brought me your hand
filled with one snail. "He'd touch anything,"
friends said the day you lifted a huge,
struggling bug to scrutinize its underside—
which is what I feared, that one day you'd reach
to touch a rattling coil, two mesmerizing eyes.

"The octopus on the platter moved."

You dream a family dinner, a platter that holds
an ocean, stacks of crab and lobster, but moving,
you sense. We talk and laugh completely unaware
they're quite alive swimming in the blue
center of our table. An octopus gluttonously reaches
for a sleeping seal. In you go, into that icy
water. We talk and laugh, you say, completely unaware.

for Bill

Feeding the Winds

Stories pass like genes through families,
like a grandmother's gold
eyes appearing again and again
as the house creaks, ages.

Stories are saved in the voice.
Stars shine in long nights, those old rivers,
and the raspy telling begins. "En tiempos pasados,"
Don Fernando Tesucún tells his grandchildren,

"my abuela told me, that the great men,
the Old Maya, had wisdom.
In the center of the milpa, their fathers taught
them to cook chicken, and heat a pot of atole.

The Lords of the Wind hear
wood chop, pot clank. The Lords
of the Wind smell sizzle and stir,
and the Lords lick their lips.

The great men, the Old Maya, burn the milpa
for planting. They throw chicken
and atole to the edges of the field. *Whooooo-ooooo*,
they call to the Lords of the Wind,

north, south, east, west, to the four corners,
they call their names,
Ah Lak'in, Ah Chik'in, Ah Nohol, Ah Xaman,
to the four Lords

who open their jaws, catch
chicken juicy on their teeth.
The Old Maya throw and trust, throw and trust
corn ears will swell green.

The corn stirs, stretches.
The wind comes, and the proud Lords roar
through the fields like jaguares
ripping corn with huge paws from the stalks, but

those swaggering Lords remember
chop and clank, sizzle and stir,
and the Lords stop on the very rim
of the milpa that fed the winds.

I tell this because my abuela told me,
as her abuelos told her, long ago,"
yawns Don Fernando Tesucún
to grandchildren now asleep in his words.

La dulcería

Released into the season
of wildflowers, zumban.
Bees burst into petal scent,
gossip rumors of sweet platters,
glazed faraway place brimming
mountains of sugary crystals.

       Zumban.

The swarm pursues an orange aroma
of pumpkins, figs, tejocote
simmering in syrups,
globes rolling in huge cauldrons
dark bubblings and brewings, gold
juices released in heat.

Bodies bumping and bruising,
zumban, hundreds fly through tree
soughings, toward leche quemada,
pause only briefly to sip
fields flowering their yellow,
spinning perfumes to the sun.

     Zumban. Zumban.

They careen down streets and round
corners, veer at last, *zum-zum*,
into la dulcería,
round fruit gleaming like jewels, slide

on *ate de guayaba*
sink into brown pools of cajeta.

                        Zumban y zumban.

Buzzing bodies nuzzle coco
and jamoncillo as la dueña
en su delantal brushes
bee bumpings with "Es la temporada,"
season of suckings and burrowings,
nectar irresistible.

A River of Women

A river of women
    softened this valley,
        hummed through the heart
        of night lulling
            babies and abuelas
                into petals of sleep.

El río de mujeres
    gathered the peach light
        of dawn for warmth like a shawl,
        slid the glow
            into the desert's roots,
                eased its greyest thirst.

The river of women
    penetrates boulders, climbs
        crags jagged as hate,
            weaves through clawing thorns
            to depths parched, shriveled
            offers ripples of hope.

Río de mujeres,
    soften our valley,
        braid through its silence
            carving your freedom
                to the song you learn
                    on your winding way.

River of women,
   stream on in this valley,
     gather all spirits,
       deepen and rise,
          sustaining your daughters
           who dream in the sun.

DESCENT

It May Be Dangerous

No sound. The child watches us
and the lake, flat as an antique mirror.

No wind, no ripples or waves,
just three of us, until the creature rises.

The child's face is my mother's.
She wears a white dress puffy with sleeves.

Or is it my daughter that gazes at me
still as a photograph from years away?

I am the middle woman,
not my mother, not my daughter.

Even when the head rises from the lake,
there are no ripples. I open my palm to it.

Its breath is warm, and I want to stroke
the long muzzle of this moose, perhaps.

I am the middle woman,
not my mother, not my daughter.

I feel what the man doesn't: the child
watches me. There are teeth in this warm mouth

and the child watches. I am the middle woman,
not my mother, not my daughter.

I am a woman standing on the edge of a lake
holding a mouth in my hand. There is no sound.

Sly Woman

The woman who hides from me is sly,
but careless in her invisibility.
She moves through my rooms at ease,
rubbing lemon oil into wood tables, cleaning
kitchen counters with a damp cloth; but I see her
signs: half cup of tea, open book,
cluster of pods and rocks, pitcher of wildflowers.

Room to room I stalk the woman
who hides
from me like I stalked
my daughter's cat
hiding to sleep indoors.
I listen with my skin.
She is sly, the woman who hides from me, but
doesn't know I feel her move with no sound down my hall.

I push the swinging door, and there, caught
in the act, her kitchen hands humming so
she doesn't hear my breath. How small
and peaceful she seems, slicing carrots
and cucumber in the sun, that old rhythm,
the drumming of a knife, sliced circles of sun

and moon, the slow pleasure
of a woman who now cooks only for herself.

My hands reach to pounce on the woman
who hides from me,
to make her look at me and see
this is *my* house, but she is sly,
and vanishes in my fingers.

Cuidado

"Humans should smell like this,"
she says, walks again into beebuzz
away from children's shouts,
   "Cuidado, Mamá,"
into sweet, thick nectar,
the very air peach
around soft, ripe fruit,
mouth open for tree's breath,
   "Cuidado,"
arms rising, slow dance
in the hot afternoon,
woman and tree,
its limbs so heavy they sway
down to her bare feet, tug
at the faded dress she lifts
away, sheds the unnecessary.

Dizzy, she rubs peachfuzz
on her lips, lets warm juice run,
smooths duraznos on face and arms,
leaves baskets and children,
drifts to her husband's frowning back,
his perfect rows of corn,
saying, "Ven. Smell. Smell."

Spring Shining

We watch him
stroke her body,
slim as a stem.

He sees us watching.

What does he think
as he rubs oil, or is it
wax, between his hands,
rubs her shoulders and back,
his strokes slow, circular,
as he moves his hands
over her curves, into her
crevices, down her
legs, rubs oil between
each toe, begins again—
facing her now—massages
her shoulders, arms,
oils her breasts as we
watch, cups them, moves his
hands down her hips, kneels
and strokes calves, thighs,
the folds between her legs,
rises, smooths ointment on her
lips, feels the molding
of her face between his hands,

the nose, downcast eyes,
even her curls now burnished.

She glows like honey
in the setting sun,
silent bronze woman
in the park, lips parted,
speaking always to herself.

There Was a Woman

Your guilt tastes bitter,
but from habit I suck
it, like the woman who starved
sucking lemons she'd pick
from the intoxicating
tree outside her window
because they were handy.

She'd slice them in two,
fragrant cups she'd suck as she peered
out her window watching
men's eyes taste
every young woman
who sauntered by.

The pale juice
dissolved her teeth.
Her smile contorted to hide
gray gums,
her words
childish in a woman's mouth.

Nunca, nunca

1

In any dark, I feel his small hands slowly rub my
legs, even here, in this apartment, I keep my
curtains closed, turn on every light,
for a duende is sly and can hide in any whisper-
ing corner, at the base of any plant. His hands
like old leaves wait for my bare legs. Even here,
I hear his breath whir when I walk quickly down the silent hall.

2

In Guatemala, he'd ride moonlight horses
outside our house, grasp their manes and spin
them round in the corral as if on a carousel gone wild.
"Oyelo," Papá muttered. "Oye al duende."
At dawn he'd disappear. Horses gasped, panted,
rolled exploding eyes, until Papá calmed them,
snipped their manes woven into a braid so tight
only scissors could unweave the work.

3

Wyoooooooo, el duende whistled from the ceiba
near our house, mountain of a tree. *Wyoooooooooooo*,
he whistled, whistled to me, the sound cool
and clear as ice. Days he'd sleep
in the tree's hum. Nights he'd spit on his fingers,
slick his hair, leap about avoiding light. Waiting,
tempt my father with a bag of gold.
"Emma," Duende crooned, "*wyoooooooooooooooo*, Emma."

4

One night, his whistle wrapped around my waist, pulled
me to the tree. Mamá shouts like a howler monkey, but I
can only move into his sound, my legs swelling, tongue
filling my mouth. One step from his fingers,
Mamá grabs my braid, slaps my face, head, legs, breaks
the spell. For days, I speak no word, hear
his whistle sweet as honeywine. Papá burns
the tree. Mamá whispers, "Nunca. Nunca. Never trust the dark."

Descent into Boca del Lagarto

With trust we enter its gaping mouth, black
as ocean bottom, hard as greed, enter
the underworld, lagarto's breath, turn
our backs on that familiar comfort, light.

We descend into batsmell. Webbed wings graze
our hair, furred creatures, eyes sucking the dark.
We move into memories of old seas, salts
settling with a sigh, hardness that blooms.

Relying on the ear, we hear drip-
drop, search for some feather of light.
Cascading formations press on our chests,
relentless accretions, cavern's stone will.

Minerals roll in this simmering silence.
They thrust and climb. In slow abandonment,
columns and castles expand while cave fish glide
contemplatively through rumors of eyes.

Pools, ojos viejos, dream jaguar-masked men,
mouths sizzling rain-chants, bribes of carved jade.
Subterranean lake and river breaths rise
and drift from this wet world as clouds.

Scorpions ignore us, in whispers stroke
a handprint so fragile we stare with one eye.
We continue, squeeze through tight openings,
climb vanishing ladders, enter stiff flames.

Gems spew in fuente encantada like startled
birdsong. We descend to spirits streaming
through glittering music of a crystal garden,
petals that hold one pure note in their mouths.

Ay. A face. Did a woman carve her face,
descend into boca del lagarto,
dig herself into immaculate rock,
eyes open to this mundo caprichoso?

The Man

1

Like faceless figures they come
from forest dark as if summoned.
Trees loom, line the sliding road,
their shoulders rounded white.

Hour after hour, hushed snow drifts
into layers, a softness that buries,
smothers, weight that snaps
branches like bones.

2

All night in the strange bed, I hear
melting, an endless murmur, dream the man
who's always there, in black
corners, lurking to unlock any door.

He hides under tidy beds,
and in the dark his hands come,
the thick fingers opening,
like soundless, hungry mouths.

3

I wake to sunshine, a crisp white
room, the now familiar water murmur
innocent as carols,
looming trees returned to their tangled roots.

The man vanishes like mist.
But he's hiding. I hear
his slow breaths, his eyes never shut,
the icy glint of a thousand angry pins.

Dear Frida

1

We're stuck on you, on thorns you press
into your swan neck, black swan, niñita
limping, stubborn, withered leg.

"Frida, pata de palo. Frida, pata de palo,"
sing-sing stones to break your bones.

You cover the skinny ankle, skirts long
even when sweat slides down your legs
like sangre, your paint, Frida.

"Pata de palo, Frida, pata de palo."

You make us taste blood that burst
everywhere, bones crushed in a bus crash,
rod shoved through you pelvis to spine.

Perfect aim, your clothes ripped away,
young swan plucked clean, skin gleaming
in the sun, blood and gold, powdered gold

bursts into air with wheels, eggs, hair, bones
and screams, wild, when you glitter
like a mangled dancer, their screams:

"¡La bailarina, la bailarina!"

2

Round your bed, she dances round
your stiff white cast, your stiff white room,
La Pelona dances round your body tomb.

Clakati clak-clak, clakati clak-clak.

Bald Death watches surgeons carve,
below your long neck—knives, needles, cut,
stitch, pinch skin together, but your body falls apart.

They mold you stiff, but you slip
out head first, escape from boring ceilings through
your fingertips, through the smell of paint.

3

You're stuck on him, Frida, on your old fat frog,
your "Sapo-Rana" croaking, *Yo, yo, yo,*
into your neck, perfect aim stroking your scars

until each opens, bleeds. How his thick lips suck
on you, your Diego, immense baby bending your
crooked spine while your babies melt and slip away.

Clakati clak-clak, clakati clak-clak.

Your dolls and hungry black monkeys
curl round your neck, watch you brand
yourself, stamp Diego right between your eyes.

We want to erase him, Frida, but we can't,
the man you love more than your own sad bones,
the hungry toad who likes a woman in each hand.

He is the sun, the moon. His flesh, warm dough,
surrounds you until you can't hear the pain,
his sweat sweet brandy on your nervous tongue.

You drink his breath heavy as a storm. Lightning
sizzles through you, pelvis to spine. His hands
stroke your hair, mold your broken pieces.

You find the ones he went to, chew lips
he kissed, hungry for some shred
of him, lick his smell on their willing breasts.

No others will do. "¡Chingado!" you cry
but try men, women, bite them so hard
they bleed, but always you taste Diego, Diego.

                   4
La Pelona Tonta dances while you paint
yourself, splatter sangre, smear breasts,
thighs, arms, hands, shirts, skirts, sheets white as milk.

Your paintings don't laugh like you do,
Frida, that laugh smelling of curses,
espinas flung at curdled faces.

She grins, La Más Pelona, at her bones
in your mirror while you soak your scars, grins
at skulls floating white in your bath, small like soaps.

Clakati clak-clak, clakati clak-clak.

Your wounds are always open, Frida.
Why can't you hide stabs, gashes, corsets?
Why can't you vomit in private, like a lady?

5

Drugged, on fire, you burst into your last show
in an ambulance. You drink, sing from your bed.
You are your art, and you make us watch you die.

Clakati clak-clak, clakati clak-clak.

Frida, pata de palo, Frida, pata de palo,
we still hear, "NO!" that mangled scream, "no!"
But La Pelona says your leg has to go.

6

Clak. In your body slides, Frida, to its last burning,
bolts up in the lick of oven's hungry tongues,
hair, your hair, around your face, crackles, blazes.

January in Cincinnati

I unlock a cold house,
quiet as its prim
neighbors, rows of women
still in long dresses,
high-buttoned shoes,
eyes downcast, lips
pressed pale, flesh
and dreams well-corseted,
backs straight,
like branches reaching for light.

Above, no blue, no cloud wisps skim
the winds, no storms tumble and growl,
no lightning flashes and burns,
no ball of light rolls the sky.
Even birds walk, unable to fly
in this gray wool.

A poinsettia, flor de noche buena, struggles
in my room, uprooted long ago from Mexico,
the compact hybrid grows to order,
unlike its sprawling relatives who peer over
any rock wall, stare at any passerby, pucker
and laugh, lips round, red tongues loud in the sun.

WHERE WE WERE BORN

Litany to the Dark Goddess

Coatlicue, Mother of All Gods,
Coatlicue, She of the Serpent Skirt,
Coatlicue, Goddess of Earth, Life, Death,
Coatlicue of Coatepec,
Teteoian, Mother of the Gods, Mother of Four Hundred Thousand,
Tlaliyolo, Heart of the Earth, Blood Giver and Blood Taker,
Tititl, Stomach Where We Were Born,
Omecihuatl, Lady of Duality,
Cihuocoatl, Woman Serpent, She of the Windowless Temple,
Yoalticitl, Goddess of Cradles, Protector of Children,
Cuaucihuatl, Eagle Woman, Woman of Claws,
Yaocihuatl, Warrior Woman, Woman of Unflinching Gaze,
Quilaztli, Sorceress, Transformer into Animals,
Toci, Our Grandmother, Woman of Wrinkled Uterus,
Teotenantzin, Beloved Mother of the Gods,
Tzizimicihuatl, Infernal Mother,
Tonantzin, Our Venerated Mother,
Tonantzin of Tepeyac, Patroness of Midwives and Healers,
Virgin
Virgin of Tepeyac, Virgin of Guadalupe,
Virgin of Roses the Color of Blood,
Goddess Who Fears No Serpent,
Goddess Who Floats on the Moon,
Goddess of Folded Hands, Goddess of Folded Body,
Hidden Goddess,
Dark Goddess of Duality,
Coatlicue, Tonantzin, Guadalupe,
Silent Pedestal Goddess,
Colonized Goddess,
Goddess of Downcast Eyes,

María full of sorrows,
Santa María llena de gracia,
Virgin of Virgins,
Mother Most Pure,
Intact Mother,
Spotless Mother,
Santísima virgen,
Spiritual Vessel,
Tower of Marble,
Rosa mística,
House of Gold,
Morning Star,
Dulce madre,
Mother of Mothers,
Mother of Hope,
María de miel,
Despierta.
Dreamer of your Many Manifestations,
Despierta.
Dreamer of Fierce Origins,
Despierta. Oyenos.
Claw through their babble,
we're straining to hear.

Cuarteto mexicano

Talk Show Interviews
with
Coatlicue the Aztec Goddess
Malinche the Maligned
The Virgin of Guadalupe
and
La Llorona: The Wailer

Coatlicue's Rules: Advice from an Aztec Goddess

Rule 1: Beware of offers to make you famous.

I, pious Aztec mother lost in housework,
am pedestaled, "She of the Serpent Skirt,"
necklace dangling hearts and hands, faceless
statue, two snakes eye-to-eye on my shoulders,
goddess of earth, also death, which leads to

Rule 2: Retain control of your own publicity.

Past is present. Women are women.
I'm not competitive and motherhood isn't
about numbers, but four hundred sons and a daughter
may be a record even without the baby.
There's something wrong in this world
if a woman isn't safe even when she sweeps
her own house, when any speck can enter even through
the eye, I'll bet, and become a stubborn tenant.

Rule 3: Protect your uterus.

Conceptions, immaculate and otherwise, happen.
Women swallow sacred stones that fill their bellies
with elbows and knees. In Guatemala, a skull dangling
from a tree whispers, "Touch me,"
to a young girl, and a clear drop
drips on her palm, disappears. Dew

drops in, if you know what I mean.
Saliva moved in her, the girl says. Moved in, I say,
settled into that empty space, and grew. Men know.
They stay full of themselves, keeps occupancy down.

Rule 4: Avoid housework.

Remember, I was sweeping, humming, actually,
high on Coatepec, our Serpent Mountain, humming loud
so I wouldn't hear all those sighs inside.
I was sweeping slivers, gold and jade, picking up
after four hundred sons who think they're gods,
and their spoiled sister. I was sweeping
when feathers fell on me, brushed my face,
first light touch in years, like in a dream.

At first, I just blew them off, then I saw
the prettiest ball of tiny plumes, glowing
green and gold. Gently, I gathered it. Oh,
it was soft as baby hair, brought back mother-
shivers when I pressed it to my skin. I nestled it
like I used to nestle them, here,
when they finished nursing. Maybe I even stroked
the roundness. I have since heard that feathers
aren't that unusual at annunciations, but I was innocent.

After sweeping, I looked in vain inside
my clothes, but the soft ball had vanished, well,
descended. I think I showed within the hour,
or so it seemed. They noticed first, of course.

Rule 5: Avoid housework. It bears repeating.

I was too busy washing, cooking, sweeping again,
worrying about my daughter, Painted with Bells,
when I began to bump into their frowns
and mutterings. They kept glancing at my stomach,
started pointing. I got so hurt and mad, I started crying.
Why do they get to us? One wrong word or look
from any one of them doubles me over,
and I've had four hundred and one, no anesthetic.
Near them I'm like a snail with no shell on a sizzling day.
They started yelling, "Wicked, wicked," and my daughter,
right there with them, my wannabe warrior boy.

The yelling was easier than the whispers, "Kill. Kill.
Kill. Kill." Kill me? Their mother?
One against four hundred and one? All I'd done
was press that feathered softness into me.

Rule 6: Listen to inside voices.

You mothers know about the baby in a family, right?
Even if he hadn't talked to me from deep inside,
he would have been special. Maybe the best.
But as my name is Coatlicue, he did.
That unborn child, that started as a ball of feathers
all soft green and gold, heard my woes, and spoke to me.
A thoughtful boy. And formal too. He said, "Do not be afraid,
I know what I must do." So I stopped shaking.

Rule 7: Verify that the inside voice is yours.

I'll spare you the part about the body hacking
and head rolling. But he was provoked, remember.
All this talk of gods and goddesses distorts.

This planet wasn't big enough for all of us,
but my whole family has done well for itself, I think.
I'm the mother of stars. My daughter's white head
rolls round the heavens each night, and my sons
wink down at me. What can I say—a family
of high visibility. The baby? Up there also, the sun,
the real thing. Such a god he is, of war unfortunately,
and the boy never stops, always racing across the sky,
every day of the year, a ball of fire since birth.
But I think he has forgotten me. You sense my ambivalence.
I'm blinded by his light.

Rules 8: Insist on personal interviews.

Past is present, remember. Men carved me,
wrote my story, and Eve's, Malinche's, Guadalupe's,
Llorona's, snakes everywhere, even in our mouths.

Rule 9: Be selective about what you swallow.

Malinche's Tips:
Pique from Mexico's Mother

My face isn't red
from blushing or lust,
flush of wild, swarming
unconstricted blood.

Tip 1: In an unfriendly country,
wear a mask.
You will see more.

I hear your sticks-and-stones:
whore, traidora, slut.
What happened to mother?

My reputación
precedes me. I come
from a long line of women
much maligned,
hija de Eva,
rumors of gardens,
crushed flowery scent
heavy as sprawling, tangled
branches, scarlet breeze
velvetmoist with petals,
piel, fruitflesh, ripe
tempting tongue,
sweet juice of
words, plural hiss
of languagessssss,

serpents,
arms tasting
apple-red, mouth
and eyes wide,
ripe legs,
ribbons of blood,
birth, you, blesséd fruit
of my warm redwomb.

Tip 2: Write
your own rumors
or hire your own historians.

They say my father,
a Náhuatl prince,
died, and my mother
remarried, of course.
We're so redhot
our skin burns
in moonlight
like our eyes, blazing
cats, blacksilk,
wickedslink.
My mother sold me,
bundled my body
off to the Maya,
women and competition
of piel, the flesh.
Prince of a father,
witch of a mother,
bruja.
Sound familiar?

Tip 3: Re-view
folklore typology
and then reread
hisstory.

Women. Snakes.
Snakes and tongues. Snake-haired
women. Loose-haired women. Loose-tongued
women. Open-mouthed women. Open
women. Whores. Mothersssss.
Virgin mothers.
Women of closed
uterus. Women
of closed
mouths. Women
of covered
hair. Women
of cloaked
bodies. Women
who crush
víboras. Women
who crush their
own tongues.
Silent women.
Altared women.

Tip 4: Alter
the altared women.

I became bilingual,
learned to roll
palabras in my mouth
just to taste them,

chew, swallow,
fruta dulce.

Eva, Sor Juana,
and I remember
words' velvet in our
mouths. We tasted
their power and red
sting, long before
"English Only," fearssss
of contagion from
tangled lenguas,
of verbal intertwinings,
like the uncontrollable
breedings of snakes.

Tip 5: Remember:
monolinguals know
about linguistics
like atheists know
about theology.

I was given to
Cortés, flesh gift,
ripe-red
gift, shared
uterus, my hair
flowing, flowing like
snakes sizzling,

like blood rivers, my tongue carrying him
and his men into a world smeared scarlet,
raping and flaming tongues devouring pages

and children's bones, fire higher than pyramids
fueled by my historic lengua, *rat-rattle* of my evil.

Tip 6: Beware
historians citing
only themselves.

But, mis hijas e hijos,
you live. I'm the proud
mother of mexicanos,
brown as I am.
Conceptions happen,
remember? But,
the blesséd fruit
of my womb spits
my name.

I hear
prostitute, puta, hooker, bitch.
Try saying mamá.

Tip 7: Watch your tongues.

I try to hold you,
to wrap my arms and hair
around my children,
to say, I am
a daughter, abused
woman, abuser,
no saint, human,
sold, slave, sexual
woman, raped
woman, invisible
translator, mother

but, no virgin,
never immaculate
enough, never
fleshless enough,
never silent
enough, my eyes—
Mexico's troubled,
buried mirror.

Tip 8: If you remove your mask,
mirror, mirror won't lie.

Look. Do you see? We.
Inseparable.

Tip 9: Children are
not bastards;
children are children.

I'm in you, in
your quips, books,
analysessssssss,
snakey sueños,
carved red
masks of your mother
long-haired for
prostitution, wantonness,
lizards on my cheeks,
creatures of land,
water, symbols
of sex and divining.

En agua, I see
your mouths and eyes

opening, my children,
like waterlilies.

Tip 10: Face it:
Hating your mother
ruins your skin.

Consejos de Nuestra Señora de Guadalupe: Counsel from the Brown Virgin

You seem surprised that I've appeared.
You gape like Juan Diego as I hovered in a cloud
that December morning above dry Tepeyac. Mortals lack faith
and imagination, fear flying. Hijas, be unpredictable.

> Como la flor de rosa.
> Como el arco iris.
> Como las nubes de gloria.
> Como la luna espléndida.

Do not be insistent. I raise neither my voice nor eyes—
yet. Bodies, even celestial, are creatures of habit.
Hijas, what we repeat becomes our nature. Beware.
Goddesses fade in and out of fashion.

> Como la flor de rosa.
> Como el arco iris.
> Como las nubes de gloria.
> Como la luna espléndida.

Names and images are converted. Now I'm moon-rider
in repose, body concealed in flowing cocoon,
hands, mouth, eyes folded, cloaked in stars.
Hijas, consistent trappings can release us for internal work.

> Como la flor de rosa.
> Como el arco iris.
> Como las nubes de gloria.
> Como la luna espléndida.

You analyze the persistence of my image, how I don't fade.
Too much analysis inhibits wisdom, hijas. You fear
flying. A muse amused, I am used everywhere, auto-shops,
buses, bars, slender mother but virgen pura, no Malinche.

> Como la flor de rosa.
> Como el arco iris.
> Como las nubes de gloria.
> Como la luna espléndida.

Hijas, beware of altars and rumors of legends.
Holy men altered me, Aztec goddess to Reina de las Américas,
pyramid to cathedral. They say I called sweet as birdsong
to Juan Diego rushing to the curling hum of holy incense.

> Como la flor de rosa.
> Como el arco iris.
> Como las nubes de gloria.
> Como la luna espléndida.

Send men clear signs. They need them, hijas.
In deserts, I favor scarlet roses. Come.
Rise. Practice solitary levitation. Rise,
but ignore halos, hovering men who look like angelitos.

> Como la flor de rosa.
> Como el arco iris.
> Como las nubes de gloria.
> Como la luna espléndida.

Hijas, value contemplation. Alone, I write
my own legends. My lines improve. Play the symbols.
I loan my cape to women in tennis shoes who fly
back and forth across the Río Grande.

Como la flor de rosa.
Como el arco iris.
Como las nubes de gloria.
Como la luna espléndida.

Listen to this buzz of litanies. Endless praise inhibits musing.
Hijas, silence can be pregnant. My voice rose like a beam
of sunlight, entered Juan. Remember, conceptions,
immaculate and otherwise, happen. He knelt, full of me.

Como la flor de rosa.
Como el arco iris.
Como las nubes de gloria.
Como la luna espléndida.

Llantos de La Llorona:
Warnings from the Wailer

Every family has one.
> Even as a child, I'd hide
and cry, *ay, ay, ay,*
> when people sneered
at my parents as if they were
> below them in some hole
of quivering vermin.

Oye: Agua santa can come from our eyes.

Early the whispers begin,
> persistent as the buzz
of litanies. Flicking tongues
> say my mother *X-tabai*
and I, *ay, ay, ay,*
> though beautiful as flaming
sunsets, are dangerous.
> We start fires
in the heart,
> and below the heart.
Nights we wander near
> sighing rivers and streams,
our hair and voices rising.

Oye: Sing to confuse the gossips.

We hide, they say, in
      evening's thickshadows,
convert ourselves into trees,
      ceibas perhaps, disguise
our voices to sound like
      wives, *ay, ay, ay*,
alter ourselves to lure innocence,
      our hair and limbs tangling
round and round, like snakes
      hugging men to death.

Oye: Know your own strength.

After the Spaniard comes,
      rumor says I begin
having babies, *ay, ay, ay*,
      conceptions, remember?
I nestle them here
      when they finish nursing.
My mother *X-tabai*
      strokes their round heads,
soft as a ball of feathers.
      We whisper cuentos,
sing *rru-rru* lullabies.

Oye: Children are not bastards
      though sometimes their fathers are.

They say I drown the babies,
      bend down with them
heavy in my arms, *rru-rru*
      release them and their gur-
glings into night water,
      or do I, *ay, ay, ay*,

begin to like the feel
        of a dagger, long and thin,
one day plunge the tongue
        into those corazoncitos
to spare them
        other piquetitos,
Maybe I grow the dagger
        gleaming like my nails in moonlight.

Oye: Be resourceful. Grow what you need.

Perhaps I want to hurt the father
        who in his story
finds a woman who makes his parents smile,
        fair like every princess,
probably thinner and *ay, ay, ay*,
        silent too, and in those days,
I'm sure a virgin,
        immaculate.

Oye: Encourage any man looking for a virgin
        vessel to bear his own child.

The story is a watery
        or bloody mess and says
I wander wailing
        ay, ay, ay, near water,
por las orillas del río,
        for the souls I've lost,
"Hijas mías" I call
        like Malinche, mad women,
madbad ghostwomen
        roaming the dark.

Oye: Sometimes raising the voice does get attention.

Not all stabbings at the truth
        are fatal, as women
will attest, you daughters of a long line
        of celestial and earthly
women, knowers of serpent
        rumors, altars, silence,
suppressed sighs.

Don't think I wail every night.
        I'm a mother, not a martyr.
But try it. I wear a gown, white,
        flowing for effect
and walk by water. Desert women
        know about survival.

Join me sometime
        for there's much to bewail,
everywhere frail, lost souls.
        We'll cry, *ay, ay, ay*.

Oye: Never underestimate the power of the voice.

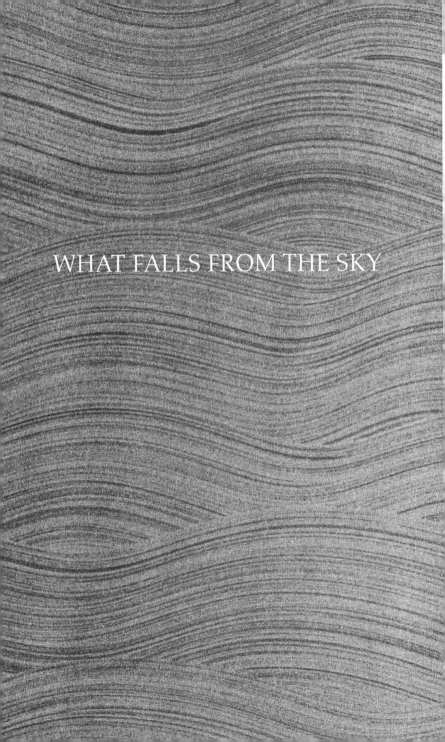

WHAT FALLS FROM THE SKY

Agua negra

I see her shadow
rocking in the candle-
light. Wind and rain bang
wood slats, slash palm trees.
We're two women caught
in a storm of stories.

In the hills, rivers
leap to light, plunge
through bougainvillea
into the green hiss,
the island's víbora.

Water rushes
down street to shacks,
to cardboard rooms. Agua negra oozes
between small toes
of shoeless children.

"I hear their whimpers,
'¡Mamá! ¡Mamá!'
from across the street,"
her voice begins its spin,
a worn familiar record,
the voice of tías and abuelitas,
storytellers.

"Ay los blanquitos
y su dinero.
Their soft hands hunger

for amber and our pink mangoes,
not the tugging
pleas, 'Look, mees. Buy, mees.'
Every afternoon
los policías grabbed
mis muchachos, threw them
into the police yard,
kicked their toothpick ribs.
No shade, no water.

'¡Mamá! ¡Mamá!' they scream,
and a club thuds a skull.
Glare scorches their eyes and throats
until turistas y su dinero sail,
hands and hearts heavy with bundles.

'¡Mamá! ¡Mamá!'

'¡Por Dios! Son niños,'
I'd yell, but they baked them
in that horno,
baked them to their bones, pobrecitos.

I bought a little house
a hiding place.
Ay, que tristeza,"
she rocks, shakes her head,
"It's our country,
and we have to hide."

Wind runs round, around
the widow's hushed home

like children chase themselves
in rain, mouths open,
ready to swallow
what falls from the sky.

Napping Sunday Afternoon

What does he dream,
este muchacho stretched out carelessly
on Sunday afternoon, how he trusts us
not to stir him from the shade.

Was it the sun that pressed him
down onto this city corner,
          pool of shade
in the noisy heat? How he trusts us

not to interrupt our tourist stroll,
bend and stroke his face,
as his mother surely did, ten years ago
wake his soft body, nest it in her arms.

How he trusts us not to taste his breath
for glue, insisting, "Muchacho, muchacho, did you?"
Did you sniff and sniff until all colors blurred again,
slid in to fill your stomach empty as a gourd?

Feet so black all hint of flesh has vanished.
He sleeps, and we step around
him, all afternoon men and women step around
the little boy asleep, not in the haystack,
                              on the street.

The Official Line

Bienvenidos, welcome, welcome, my honored guests,
to Honduras, a lush haven for you clever investors.
As we drive through the countryside, you will see
color and beauty: families, birds, fruit. Note
the banana trees, our edible gold, the rattle of exotic
leaves and the promise of sweetness ripening
in its safe peel. Like your money can.
Those? Of course, they are houses. Clever, no?
The spaces between the twigs allow air to circulate.
Our air is abundant, and we do not discriminate.
Yes, perhaps, mosquitoes pool in the crowded rooms,
but look, there, cattle and children roaming
the low hills. Pastoral, no?
The smell? Well, yes, perhaps the hills are mounds
of refuse and discarded plastic, but colorful, no? Note
the pleasure when the Lord's tame creatures fill
their mouths, perhaps one of our sweet
Honduran bananas. And birds, see? Above these tame heads,
birds circle. Buzzards, you say? Perhaps, but note
the beauty of their silhouettes against our sky.
Ah, observe the ingenuity of the Honduran peasant.
With a few wooden boxes, and bedsheets for walls,
they thrive. Note the beauty of that naked child
against the trees. Day or night, nothing separates
these people from our abundant air. They sleep
beneath our wide Honduran sky. Yes, even in the rain.
Mis compañeros, you do not understand
the Honduran soul. Come. On to a tropical lunch, ripe
hostesses, sweet-talk of money's hum.

Los brazos del río

1

"Brincaron aquí," the guide says,
wakes us from the tangle
of roots and dreams
in el Cañón del Sumidero.
Our bodies grumble again
at returning to land,
our joints reluctant
to support our weight.
We climb out of el río,
tear rotted leaves from our bones,
begin to laugh,
help one another stand,
see eyes stare through us
as we climb el cañón
to the rhythm of story,
climb back into that moment.

2

Rumor circles our village
like a buzzard. My baby sleeps
on my back while I gather berries
like my mothers, the day we smell
them, see the gleam that shatters
trees, rocks, old skeletons; pierces
us, the story true, creatures with four legs,
bodies shining head to toe,
skin clanking, legs drumming toward us,
no place to run,
only the jump

into this cañón
steep as fear
away from creatures
with thorny teeth
who press their hard skin into
women who never walk again, monstruos
howling sounds no one understands,
"Indios, indios, indios,"
slashing tongues if we cry out.

We smell them. Their mouths like caves.
Their shouts, bleached bats, chase us, tangle
in my hair. We run, run again toward the cliff,
hear our hearts now, racing like deer too wounded
to see the edge of the earth. Again, I grab my baby, fling
hard so the cliff won't cut her, so she'll fall straight into
los brazos del río. I throw myself, again.

3

The story ends.
The tourists, mouths open, stare up at us as we
fall, straining to see or hear our legs, arms,
skulls crash back into our watery grave.

I dream the creatures never came,
that I am a wrinkled woman
surrounded by grandchildren
who collect wild seeds with me,
that daily I tell my daughter,
"*Ay. Ay*. Don't let them near the edge.
Watch the children."

Fe Tzotzíl

Safe in her turquoise rebozo,
she deciphers stars, roots, wind,
retells cuentos scented by
woodsmoke, tales of tortugas,
crabs, and fish swimming above trees,

traces words written by
golondrinas, listens to chirps
for rain, feels tomorrow
in her palms, safe
en su rebozo turquesa,

throws dry corn to hear
its secretos like the eyes
crouched near her for warnings,
follows her fingers
trembling above unseen streams
deep below her feet, flowing
as purple ribbons
meander down her braids.

She brings hope
in jars to water gods,
releases blossoms
into mariposas,
corn leaves into
pájaros verdes,

runs through crystal
ribbons of rain, segura

en su rebozo turquesa,
through the tunnel
of gunbarrels, through
the eyes of soldiers,
sombras de ceniza,
to scarred wood doors,
weave of drums, smoke, flutes,
altar sailing in incense,
segura en su rebozo turquesa.

Carpet of pine needles pricks her feet,
carpet of candles flutters, alas blancas,
her chanting
na-na-na-na-na-na-na,
holds a bandaged hand,
guides it over eggs, *posh*,
to bring the limp man a wife,
young, full of babies,
segura en su rebozo turquesa,

prays: take them away, los soldados,
sombras de ceniza,

hears the mirrors on the robes
San Martín, Teresita, La Virgen,
Santo Niño de Atocha,
ribbons streaming,
spirits flowing,
her lips on their feet cold as wet stone,
smoke and mirrors,
entre sombras de ceniza, the Cross,
His face white as bleached bone,
her arms wide, chanting

na-na-na-na-na-na-na,
blood, streaming red ribbons
down cheeks, arms, legs,
His holy feet blooming red
wounds in her hands,
segura en su rebozo turquesa,
entre sombras de ceniza,
His skin white as bleached bone,
cold as wet stone on her lips,
like the glass casket,
His head wrapped in thorns
on alas blancas, eyes closed,

runs through crystal
ribbons of rain, gunbarrels, tunnel of eyes,
segura en su rebozo turquesa,
entre sombras de ceniza.

Tzimin Chaak

Rise, Sweet Horse, gather your resting bones.
Let me hold your breath hot in my hands.
I've brought you the freshest grasses,
purple tart petals, hay spiced with wind.

When El Cortés left you, our first horse,
our hearts pounded louder than your hoofs.
We fed you our beans, chicken, tortillas.
You stamped, snorted. One day, your teeth stopped.

But didn't I come to you, Sweet Horse?
Didn't I stroke your long face and flank?
I knew your yellow teeth could chew my flesh,
but I put out my hand, brimming berries.

Why did you let flies swim in your swollen eyes?
Why did you let our food rot in your mouth?
Why did you lie down, let your life leak out?
Why did you die, Sweet Horse, why did you?

I sang to you when we were alone.
I covered you with leaves, boiled herbs.
I danced around you, rattled rattles
spooking spirits chewing on your heart.

I did what a girl could, my Sweet Horse.
Buzzards high in the sky called your name.
Our elders pounded their palms with frowns,
plotted stories for Hernán Cortés.

Remember the honey, Sweet Horse?
I closed my eyes in that spinning tree,
climbed into the gold buzzing, a smell
thick as the dripping amber I stole.

I hoped the warm stream of sun would slide
down your throat, tasting of wildflowers,
of cold dew at dawn, heal you, Sweet Horse,
so that we could leap into the wind.

Trembling men buried you, then crossed the lake,
carved a rock horse. An old *aj waay*
blew his breath into the rock's cold mouth
until the stone stirred; its eyes opened.

Tzimin chaak, a thunder beast, thudded
to the lake, sailed to us, but sailed into
a pounding storm, waves taller than these trees.
Enormous, the horse sank into a roar.

My people's shame shows; they dread Cortés.
It's you I miss. Return, Sweet Horse. Rise,
carry me above treetops. We'll fly,
you and I, gallop wild with the wind.

Tornabé

Waves swell warm as mothermilk,
undulate green beneath hills of Honduras.
Tornabé on the sand by the sea.

Boys splash in small lagoon, laughter rising
sunward, careless kites. Palms gossip,
arms arching into wind.

    Tornabé on the sand by the sea.

Down dirt paths, by slatted wood houses,
thatched roots, pecking eyes of dogs, roosters, children;
head-scarves hum the islands.

    Tornabé on the sand by the sea.

"Buenas tardes," la Garífona says bending for centuries
into smell of bread, into tin heat, makeshift oven,
smolder of rocks, coconut shells.

    Tornabé on the sand by the sea.

Black arms lift mountains, raise blazing slab,
bread browning under trees. Hot round puffs
sweet with coconut oil dissolve on tongue.

Tornabé on the sand by the sea.

Under clouds dark with greed, la Garífona dreams
with the sea: her granddaughter dancing in *mua*'s breath
to drum's old pulse. Tornabé on the sand by the sea.

Depression Days

He buys the dark
                    with his last fifteen cents.
Reel after reel, he's on the deck with men
who fill their chests taut on the high seas,
who boom, "Red Sails in the Sunset."

He tries not to think
                    of last night on his cot,
his private reel, border kid playing CCC lumberjack,
gripping an ax, slicing the green
pine scent in a house dark from his father's death.

He tries not to think
                    of the men who climbed
cold on the truck with him that morning,
"¡Caramba, qué frío!" Their stomachs
screechy as gears, hungry for paychecks.

He tries not to think
                    of the desert wind sliding
into the barracks, herding bare flesh
around the stove's warm belly. "Am I alive, doc?"
his joke limp as his clothes bag.

He tries not to think
                    of the sergeant
spitting, "DELGADO." My uncle steps forward
into a frown. "I SAID DELGADO."
"I am Delgado." The twitch of lips. The wind.

He tries not to think
                                of the words later.
"You don't look Mexican, Delgado.
Just change your name," (his formal father
eyeing him) "and you've got a job."

He buys the dark
                                with his last fifteen cents.
He tries not to think of the bare icebox, his mother's sighing
eyes, of his father who never understood
this country, of the price of eggs and names and skin.

                                                for Eduardo Delgado

Cuban Revolutionary

José hears colors. A shirtless boy
from the fields, he watches painters
at el taller when he sweeps
their spattered floor, listens.

    Oye verde, oye azul.

He walks the streets of Havana hearing
the blare of a girl's skirt whirl red,
purling of light on a dove's creamy feathers,
clamor of the island's canary sun.

    Oye verde, oye azul.

The artists watch Jose's eyes,
listening. He begins mixing the jade sough
of sea pines with silver lisp of waves, orange hibiscus
fanfare with black pad of cat stalking its shadow.

    Oye verde, oye azul.

He paints, hardly hears money's racket, hard boots
stomping, speakers blasting: ¡Yanqui Imperialistas!
bar music rippling down the street
from days when Papa H. strolled with his compañeros.

    Oye verde, oye azul.

Che's flags flap in the heat. José, gray now
but still shirtless, sweats over his work, says
he loves it, all he knows how to do for la Revolución,
returns to his canvas, its echoes of blue.

Oye verde, oye azul.

Doña Feliciana

Ven. Come inside. Es mi casa,
two rooms I built from wood scraps.
Look at the nails, bent como mis dedos.
They spilled us like garbage,
the landowners with the big trucks, spilled us
in this bare field with our pots, sheets,
shoes stiff and old as tree bark.

At first, niños raced across the land,
gulping in all the new, wide air.
They ran laughing into the emptiness,
no trees, no mangoes and avocados lying in the shade,
no houses, no plastic water buckets,
no tomato plants, no small fires, no gallinas,
nothing, no thing in their way.

I brought just one plant, a little cilantro,
placed it in this blue tin pot. Smell it,
even a little green helps in all this dust.
Es mi casa. I am my family, widow
without children. Mis compañeros and I have no land,
not even a stream of water thin as a thread.

The first nights in this bare place, mosquitoes
sucked and sucked until I had to build a house.
Alone, at sixty-three. My arms hurt from dragging
boards. My head ached from banging,
but I lifted my house up, made myself a roof.
See? Two rooms: here I sleep, here I cook arroz.

Nights I lie in the dark and listen to the wind,
whisper to my viejo, "I did it.
I built myself a house.
I hung my blue tin pot beside my door."

Mangos y limones

The story is about swellings and slick slidings,
about bodies that grow and others that slide out
wet, like mangos, gold flesh fermenting in saltwater,
about a woman biting into the salty juice alive
on her tongue, filling her mouth, piece after piece
until, in a small kitchen, she finishes the jar,
smiling and chewing in silence,
her friend's eyes open as wells.

The story is about daughters
and what they know of the dark,
her youngest who feels the unseen,
what the woman doesn't, her body,
casual in its bleedings, this time no curdling
when she eats tortillas y queso blanco warmed in the sun.
"*Ay* los hombres," she concludes, "they're different
even before a speck of them is visible."

The story is about lemons, twenty-five tart moons
she digs into salt, chewing lemon after lemon,
lips hungry, open, unlike that youngest daughter,
lips shut for months, eyes smaller,
smaller as the mother's body swells, the girl who runs
into the room at the first cry, presses the baby,
slick as peeled fruit, to her breast, says, "You
were killing me. Mami, I suffered. Es mío."

The mother thinks of them back in El Salvador,
when she slices limones or peels mangos.
Yellow scents pucker her memory,

her mouth then and its cravings, the aching
for fruit and hunger for grains of sweet salt. Her body
thicker now, she slides a slice of mango between her lips,
laughs about once eating twenty-five frosted lemons,
her mouth full of her own stories.

Desert Mockingbird

Even on Sunday,
you advertise your disrespect.

In this age of diplomacy,
you're a true smart mouth

belting out crazy combinations
with no careful qualifiers,

sass without a future,
brash, tactless, no bureaucrat.

Indifferent to all frowns,
you play sounds,

and when you stop
only cicadas throb, doves coo.

All year I wait for you,
a tease I can't resist

tempting me to throw my head back
and just let the sounds slide up
                         and out

La Migra

1

Let's play La Migra.
I'll be the Border Patrol.
You be the Mexican maid.
I get the badge and sunglasses.
You can hide and run,
but you can't get away
because I have a jeep.
I can take you wherever
I want, but don't ask
questions because
I don't speak Spanish.
I can touch you wherever
I want but don't complain
too much because I've got
boots and kick—if I have to,
and I have handcuffs.
Oh, and a gun.
Get ready, get set, run.

2

Let's play La Migra.
You be the Border Patrol.
I'll be the Mexican woman.
Your jeep has a flat,
and you have been spotted
by the sun.
All you have is heavy: hat,
glasses, badge, shoes, gun.
I know this desert,

where to rest,
where to drink.
Oh, I am not alone.
You hear us singing
and laughing with the wind,
Agua dulce brota aquí, aquí, aquí,
but since you can't speak Spanish,
you do not understand.
Get ready.

WONDROUS WETNESS

Pescadote

What think you, Old Fish,
mammoth, mud-stuck
for centuries, your scales
spinning long ago
like tiny chimes
calling fishermen
who slipped the silver
under their pillows,
dreamed of swimming
with immense starfish
in the silk night sky.

What think you, Old Fish,
your flesh nibbled
by river breezes
that licked even your wild
eyes away, your moon
bones thickening, expanding
with wet burrowings,
fins and tendrils skimming
your ribs, roots curling
into damp crevices.

What think you, Old Fish,
spiders lacing
your gray crust, by light
of fireflies, spinning
slow stories on you,
lone river island

unmoved by torrents.
Trees sprout from your head
humming, at sunset,
your mouth open
to the gathering wind.

Metamórfosis

Pearls here
Pearls there
Pearls behind us
—GEORGE SARANDÁRIS

I

Topless,
she rules
her turquoise sea,
this child,
kicks her commands.

Arms outflung,
she orchestrates
waves, enters
her Aegean kingdom,
plants her small
feet triumphantly
on obedient sand,
scolds a swell
that lifts her
with its clear power.

The sea bows,
retreats.
Vasílissa
tis thálassas
smiles
regal approval
at the light
rippling of her long mysterious hair.

II

Laughing, full nude
   fengári tosses
an eager string
   of fish to cheer
the night-brooding sea.

Like fireflies, they dart
   and glint in the sea's dark,
whispering folds.
   The fish leap
to ride the waves
   of its silver sorrow
like stars scurrying
   to our fabled shores.

Might I step softly
   on the jasmine shimmer
of their fins
   from island to island,
on this fragrant bridge of light?

III

We are all beautiful
   in water. Girls
      lift their mothers
         laughing in their arms.
Grandmothers, heavy in sand,
   float in this
      caressing sea,
         point their toes, dancers again,

their arms, graceful, as silvery-
   green olive trees,
      their legs, lovely in play,
         in ripples of light.

Sueño de miel

Clear as sun-
light streams
through years,
travels orchards,
brews pale juice
of pears, streams
through bird-
song, mists,
rivers, honeysuckle,
scents braided
by drowsy
wind, recounts
dreams abuzz
with lips too hard
to read, turned faces—
sound flows, slow
thread, amber
pollen-sweet
slides gold
into our inked symbols,
black on white,
miel streaming
in a patient
ear.

El Río Grande

Maybe La Llorona is el Río Grande
  who carries voices wherever she flows,
the voices of women who speak only Spanish,
  who hold their breath, fluttering
like a new bird, cupped in their own hands high
  above their heads.

Maybe La Llorona is el Río Grande
  who rolls over on her back some afternoons
and gazes straight into the sun,
  her hair streaming brown into fields of onion
and chile, gathering voices of women who laugh
  with their own fear.

Maybe La Llorona is el Río Grande
  who penetrates even granite, gathers the stars
and moon and tells her cuentos all night long,
  of women who scoop her to them in the heat,
lick her on their lips, their voices rising
  like the morning star.

Let Us Hold Hands

Let us now hold hands
with the Iroquois woman who slipped berries into children's lips
while her sisters planted stars with a wooden hoe,

with the woman who rubbed warm oil into her neighbor's feet
when Plymouth's winter prowled and howled outside their doors,

with the woman who sewed faith into each stitch, cloth comforts
pieced to the rhythm of español for babies born al silencio del desierto,

with the woman who seasoned soups with pepper and hope
as her days took her further from sighs of trees she loved,

with the woman who parted her parched lips and sang
for her mother when they staggered onto these shores in chains,

with the woman who trained her stubborn tongue to wrap
around that spiny language, English, to place her child in school.

Let us now hold hands with the woman
who croons to the newborn left amid orange rinds and newspaper,
who teaches grandmothers to knit letters into a word, a word,
who whispers to the woman dying with one breast,
who holds a wife whose face is more broken than any bone,
who bathes the woman found sleeping in black snow.

Let us hold hands
with the woman who holds her sister in Bosnia, Detroit, Somalia,
Jacksonville, Guatemala, Burma, Juárez, and Cincinnati,

with the woman who confronts the glare of eyes and gunbarrels,
yet rises to protest in Yoruba, English, Polish, Spanish, Chinese, Urdu.

Let us hold hands
with the woman who cooks, with the woman who builds,
with the woman who cries, with the woman who laughs,
with the woman who heals, with the woman who prays,
with the woman who plants, with the woman who harvests,
with the woman who sings, with the woman whose spirits rise.

In this time that fears faith, let us hold hands.
In this time that fears the unwashed, let us hold hands.
In this time that fears age, let us hold hands.
In this time that fears touch, let us hold hands,
brown hands, trembling hands, calloused hands, frail
hands, white hands, tired hands, angry hands, new
hands, cold hands, black hands, bold hands.

In towns and cities and villages, mano a mano, hand in hand,
in mountains and valleys and plains, a ring of women circling
the world, the ring strong in our joining,
around our petaled home, this earth, let us hold hands.

Un cuento de agua santa

The king frowned, of course,
lonely, we say, moving in his flowing robes
through the world's dark,
no trees rustling, no waves whispering,
a black, brittle place, this earth.
Humans used their hands
as eyes, closed their fingers
in sleep, dreamed a haloed place,
streams of light.
Poets wrote of its soul,
and mothers let their babies
teethe to round songs of its sound.

Brood he did, el rey high
in the gloomy heavens, slumped
on his throne, hoarding his
secrets in three vessels of clay.
One day, while he slept,
a woman, not that young, played
with the impish guards,
the celestial grasshoppers, until
they lifted the lid from the first,
immense cántaro de barro.

Light curled out like incense,
drifted down canyons,
bounded up mountains leaping
rock to rock. The rays rolled
and rose into a round blaze
waking the king

who for the first time saw
flesh, feather, fur.
The creatures of the earth
gazed up, mouths and eyes wide
for days. All throats—eagle,
bear, child, dry in amazement.
The earth was silent
and thirsty.

The king pondered
on his throne
in his flowing robes
while the woman coaxed
the leaping specks
of light to lift
the second lid.
She dipped her finger
into the agua santa

slid both hands into
a fluid she remembered
but had never known,
and then, with her hip
tipped that cántaro
de barro and poured
crystal ribbons from the sky.

Humans raised their arms
to clasp the strange and
wondrous wetness.
They walked on water.
Seeds burst and pines and palms stretched
to the sun. Pink plumes of sugar

cane towered over mountains.
The water sculpted caves
and grottos, curved into
rivers, pooled in oceans.

The water rose
and rose.
The king frowned
but in his flowing robes,
he only brooded.
The woman lifted
the heavy cántaro de barro.
She teased the chapulines
to lift the final lid.

A breeze curled out
loosening her hair.
Winds swooped, gathered
mounds of mists
into clouds.

At the long day's end,
the woman's body ached,
and she burrowed into
the luscious dark.
She dreamed
earth rested on the shell
of a green turtle floating
on the waves of the old sea.
Souls, white and perfumed
gardenias, bloomed
on the tree of life.
They drifted

into bones and skin,
scenting bodies from within.
When the bodies loosened,
the souls slid
down into the underworld,
la tierra oscura,
and bloomed wet again, again, and again.

Agio Neró

Here, in this mineral landscape
of rock and sea . . .
in a dazzling flash you may stare
    at your true self.
—ALEXANDER MÁTSAS

Finding a spring, a holy act,
    in a land of rocks.
Priests built shrines to house
    sweet, transparent waters.
Pilgrims slipped eager hands
    into crystal streams,
rubbed *ágio neró*
    into their faces and lips,
then cupped their hands
    with care to sip the healing flow.

Hearts still as stones
    remembered the rhythm of the sea.
Black spirits burst
    from pilgrims' twisted lips,
Ragged wounds sealed themselves
    smooth as apricots.
Limp tongues quivered
    to life praising, holy, holy, holy.

At Kefalári, they say
    that Leon, emperor of Byzantium,
when young wandered

by their cave.
He met a blind old man
    thirsting for shade and drink.
Panaghía's voice above said,
    "All you need is here."

Leon led the old man
    to refreshing water.
The man washed
    tired wrinkles from his face,
scooped the sacred
    to his cracked, dry lips and drank,
his sigh deep as the black sighs
    of the midnight sea.

A round, shining host rose.
    The old man saw light.

Under wisteria cascade, we enter
    that cave's mouth.
Candles flicker gold in
    lamps near an icon,
María and her sweet child
    in a fountain.
Water beads from her shawl
    into clear, precious jewels,
flows to the faithful
    below like this spring flows
from an old pipe
    into our curious hands,
or into small, plastic bottles
    sold in the cave's chapels,
portable holiness;

baptismal font, snipping
of hair, cutting the tie
   with Adam and Eve,
old sin, sacred oil,
   child totally immersed
in holy water,
   agua santa, *ágio neró*.

At Hághia Moní nuns in black
   hear splashing,
their sacred spring
   also spilling from an old pipe
to goldfish and gardens,
   zinnias, pomegranates,
lemon and orange trees,
   aroma of incense
and innocence, for this spring
   is Kánathos,
here Hera bathed, renewing
   her virginity,
where pious nuns polish gold
   kandília in the dark
with the gray flowing
   of their holy, holy beards.

Roosters startle drowsing waters.
   Old women nod
kaliméra, kaliméra,
   daily music, like the splashing
of oleanders, geraniums, bougainvillea,
   by these hands that boil bones,
their loved ones,

in dark wine, for re-burial,
a holy blood.

Sun lights white mountaintop
    chapels, the Profétis Elías,
holy spaces, solitary beacons of faith.

Anxious women enter
    the dark. They light thin tapers
that sway in the soughing
    of morning wind, flickering
memory of chanting.
    Women fill clear votive cups
with oil and longing
    to be filled,
rub the wet promise into their skin.
    Surely alone, they rub
agua santa into their abdomens,
    smooth and warm
as dough they glaze
    to rise in the aroma of oranges.

Near the village,
    sheep bow their heads,
silence broken by the ringing
    of their bells
and by digging, again the search
    for water.

Archaeologists at Mikínes and Midéa
    piece vessels that once held oil,
olives, wine, perfume, water,

hands faithful
though wary of faith,
   drinking pure, bottled water,
climbing through wild oregano,
   sage and thyme,
to enter dark
   cisterns, carved
into limestone by those who
   slept with the sea, knew her
moody mystery.
   They enter
tight, dark openings
   shaped like almonds, come
seeking old springs, a taste
   honey-sweet on the tongue.

They stare down wells,
   ponder mountains dripping
stone and water, rock's sweet tears,
   pooling like an eye of God.
They read sherds, vessels—
   amphora, krater, kylix—
and bones, lonely like ours,
   holy vessels.

Children are we, of the sacred
   sapphire sea.
Holy, holy, holy.

Cuentista

She carries a green river
in her arms, a rolling play of light.
"En tiempos pasados" she whispers,
"waves of the old sea crested, rose
on these stern mountains. Over this sand,
fish and stars swam."

Ripples and fins stream
silver on and in our skin. Our bones sway.
"The land dried. Crawl into caves,
dark,
damp as owlmouth.
Still, agua santa echoes."

At night, fish stream
through her hair, water fronds.
The whisper of scales,
a muted song, vanishes in sunlight,
like the stars.

She carries a green river,
heavy, but it hums.
In any desert, she can bow her head
and sip from her own arms.

Notes

"Ofrenda for Lobo": On November 2, Mexicans observe the Day of the Dead. A traditional aspect of the observance is the creation of tiered altars, ofrendas, designed to lure deceased relatives by means of their favorite dishes and objects.

"Corazón del corrido": A corrido is a border folk ballad. An aspect of this traditional form is the hero on a horse, pistol in hand.

"Mama Spell": A nagual is an alter or guardian animal spirit.

"Dear Frida": La Pelona was feisty Frida's name for death.

"Coatlicue's Rules: Advice from an Aztec Goddess": In Aztec mythology, Coatlicue is the mother of Huitzilopochtli, the sun god, who is born fully armed. He slays his sister, Coyolxauqui, Painted with Bells, who becomes the moon, and his four hundred brothers, Centzón Huitznahua, who become the stars.

"Llantos de La Llorona: Warnings from the Wailer": In Mexican and Southwest legends, La Llorona is a weeping woman who wails at night, often near water, for her dead children. *X-tabai* is also a night-wandering woman in Maya legends who is rumored to lure men to their death.

"Fe Tzotzíl": The Tzotzíl are a Maya group living in Chiapas. *Posh* is a Maya word for cane liquor.

"Tzimin Chaak": *Tzimin* means horse and *aj waay* means shaman in the Itzaj Maya language spoken in Guatemala.

"Tornabé": *Mua* means land in Garífona, the language of Blacks at Tornabé who came to Honduras from San Vicente over two hundred years ago. The Garífona struggle to retain their lands, language, and culture.

"La Migra": This term is used along the United States/Mexican border for United States Immigration agents.

"Metamórfosis": In Greek, *vasílissa tis thálassas* means queen of the sea. *Fengári* is the moon.

"Agio Neró": These words mean holy water in Greek. *Panaghía*, meaning all holy, is another name for Mary. *Kandilia* are oil lamps, and *kaliméra* means good morning.

ABOUT THE AUTHOR

Pat Mora, award-winning poet whose most recent collection is *Adobe Odes,* has also written many children's books. Her books of nonfiction include *House of Houses* and *Nepantla: Essays from the Land in the Middle*. She lives in Santa Fe, New Mexico.